Gardener's Guide to t]

A Botany Handbook About th

Gardeners' Guide to Botany Series - Book 2

Paul R. Wonning

Gardener's Guide to the Plant Root

Published By Paul R. Wonning

Copyright 2016 by Paul R. Wonning

Print Edition

paulwonning@gmail.com

If you would like email notification of when new Mossy Feet books become available email the author for inclusion in the subscription list.

Mossy Feet Books

www.mossyfeetbooks.com

Description

Gardener's Guide to the Plant Root is a basic beginning or veteran gardener's botany guide to the plant root.

The root system of the plant is essential to its survival as it gathers water, nutrients and anchors the plant in the soil. This botany guide serves as a handbook to the plant root and introduction to basic botany. Use it to learn about the plant root and root systems that the plant depends upon for survival.

Paul R. Wonning

Table of Contents

Gardener's Guide to the Plant Root

Paul R. Wonning

Chapter 1 The Plant Root - Introduction

Of the three major organs of a plant, the root is the most inconspicuous due to its existence underground. The root, or radical, is the first organ to appear when the seed germinates. Its first function is to anchor the developing seedling in the soil and take in water and nutrients from the soil. These functions, with the addition of becoming a food storage area for the plant, remain the primary functions of the root for the lifetime of the plant.

Tap Root

Depending upon the type of plant the radical will develop into one of two major root systems, the tap root system or the fibrous system. Monocots like grasses tend to develop fibrous root systems. Many dicots like carrot and some trees have a tap root system. The fibrous root system of grasses resists the upward pressure of animals as they graze on the leaves and prevent it from uprooting as the animal feeds. Taproot systems for the larger plants help anchor taller plants like trees, in the soil. Most trees will also develop fibrous roots also to help anchor them and gather water and nutrients over a wider area.

Fibrous Root

The root has developed various specialized tissues to aid it in its functions. These tissues are root hair, epidermis, epiblem, cortex, endodermis, pericycle and the vascular tissue. Generally, the root hairs, using a process called osmosis, absorb water, nutrients and minerals from the soil. The root hairs transfer these materials to the vascular area that transports them to the rest of the plant for use. Legumes like peas and beans grow specialized structures called nodules that, in association with certain specialized bacteria, provide nitrogen for the plants use.

Roots grow from the tip using a group of specialized cells called the root cap to protect the root itself during growth. The roots will grow in any direction in the soil that satisfied their needs for moisture, nutrients and minerals.

Many plants have developed a specialized stem or bud structure that is often mistaken for roots. Gladioli have a specialized stem called a corm, which grows underground, and the root system emanates outward from the bottom of the corm. Potatoes have enlarged buds called tubers that grow underground. These tubers are really a specialized stem, not a root.

Many roots like carrots, beets, horseradish and sweet potatoes are important food sources for humans and have enormous commercial value.

The roots, or parts of roots, of many plant species have become specialized to serve adaptive purposes besides the two primary functions described in the introduction.

Back to Table of Contents

Chapter 2 Anatomy of the Root

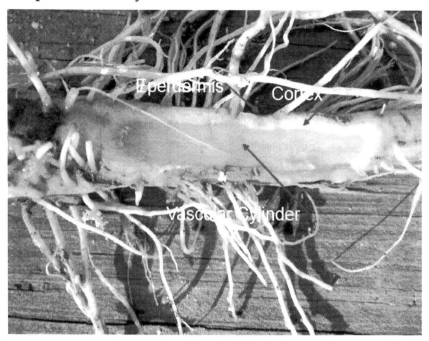

Most plant roots are composed of five main areas. These parts of the roots are the root tip, epidermis, cortex, xylem and phloem.

The root cap is located at the very tip of the root. It is a thimble shaped structure that serves to protect the root tip, or apical meristem, which is composed of almost continuously growing cells.

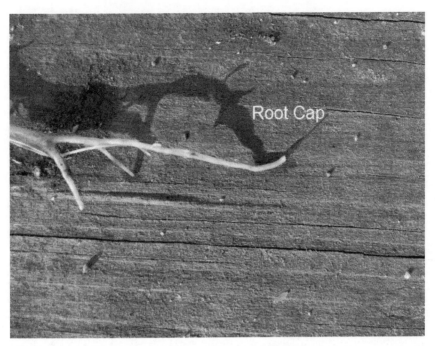

Root Cap

The epidermis is the skin of the root, composing its outmost surface. It is a single cell thick in most plants and it serves two functions, to protect the tissues within the root and to allow minerals and water to pass through. Microscopic root hairs grow outward from some of the cells of the epidermis, greatly expanding the surface area of the root and increasing the amount of minerals and roots that may be taken in.

The next layer of the anatomy of a root is the cortex. The parenchyma cells and the endodermis make up the cortex. Parenchyma cells mostly serve as storage structures and these are where excess food produced in the plant's leaves are stored for future use. The endodermis is the innermost layer of the cortex. A waxy substance called the Casparian strip surrounds each cell, forcing minerals to pass through the cells of the endodermis by a process called osmosis, and not around them. This limits the amount of minerals and water passing into the cortex.

The vascular cylinder is the innermost layer of the plant root. It is composed of two structures, the xylem and the phloem. Both layers are composed of tube shaped cells and both have similar functions, the transportation of materials from one area of the plant to another. The xylem is composed of dead, tubular cells called veins, whose purpose is to transport minerals and waters to the stem and then on to the leaves, sort of like a pipe system within the plant root. The cells of the phloem are living cells, also tubular in shape and referred to as sieve tubes. The phloem also acts like a pipeline system, moving food either manufactured in the leaves to for immediate use or stored in the cortex for future use.

The way the system functions is simple in concept. The root hairs take in water and minerals and pass it into the cortex. Pressure builds up, forcing them through the endodermis, into the phloem, and from there up into the stem and outward to the leaves.

Chapter 3 Adventitious Root

The definition of the word adventitious is something that is accidentally acquired or not inherent. Adventitious roots are roots that have their origin in plant tissues other than the root tissue. They are not inherent to the tissue that they arise from as they originate in tissue that is above ground. Adventitious roots can originate from the stem, leaf or even old, woody tissue and are actually quite common in the plant world. Ground ivy usually forms small root tips on the joint of the leaf and stem. English ivy forms adventitious roots along the stem and these roots help anchor the plant to trees or buildings when the plant climbs. If a soil covers a portion of the stem, many plants have the ability to form adventitious roots. Indeed, this is the method for a method of plant propagation called layering.

Adventitious roots usually develop near the vascular tissue and connect the phloem and xylem. The plants ability to form adventitious roots is very important for plant propagators. Adventitious roots that form on the base of the cutting form a new plant, or clone, of the plant. The act of cutting the plant seems to stimulate root formation, as many times roots will form on the callus that forms at the cut end of the cut stem. The plant propagator can sometimes stimulate root formation quicker using additional wounding near the base of the cutting or plant applying rooting hormones.

Chapter 4 Aerial Roots

Aerial roots are a type of non-parasitic, adventitious root that forms above ground and stays above ground. An aerial root will usually form on the stem or the base of a leaf. Some aerial roots, like those of the English Ivy, Virginia Creeper and poison ivy help the vine cling to trees or other hard surfaces that they want to climb. These aerial roots end in a flat, suction cup shaped appendage that clings tightly to whatever surface it manages to adhere.

Some aerial roots, like those that grow on orchids, actually have the ability to absorb water from the atmosphere. These roots develop a hard outer shell of dead cells called the velamen. These roots hang down into the damp, humid air and absorb whatever water they can from the air. The velamen is spongy, white and gives the root a silvery appearance. It will cover the entire root except the tip of the aerial root, which is green.

Chapter 5 Aerating Roots

An aerating root is a root that arises above the water line on trees that grow in water like cypress and mangrove trees. Roots on these trees typically form protuberances that grow upwards and extend several inches above the waterline. In some tree species there are specialized cells that allow the exchange of oxygen between the atmosphere and the root.

Aerating roots, called knee roots, or pneumatophores. In cypress trees, there is no known function for the knee, as it does not seem to aid in gathering oxygen from the air. The aerating roots of the mangrove help to stabilize soil and provide habitat for wildlife in the areas that the tree grow in. The extensive root system of the mangrove also helps to provide a barrier against the heavy winds of cyclones. Cultivation of mangrove trees along the coast of many Southeast Asian courtiers for this purpose is common.

Most plants with aerating roots have their homes in swampy or wetland locations. Trees that develop aerating roots include:

Glyptostrobus

Bald Cypress

Pond Cypress

Ahuehuete

Metasequoia

Back to Table of Contents

Chapter 6 Contractile Roots

Some plants, as the stem grows, have the tendency to work themselves upwards and out of the soil. To combat this, these plants have developed a specialized root called a contractile root. This type of root is common in the magnolia and lily family but it is also present in many other plants as well. Many seedlings also possess contractile roots that serve to keep the plant at the proper soil depth during the rapid growing phase that follows germination. Many plants with rhizomes or bulbs have a tendency to grow out of the ground. A whorl of contractile roots around the upper portion of the bulb keeps them at the proper depth.

Wrinkling in the middle portion of the contractile root is common, though just before the contracting phase the center portion of the plant may swell. Many think that prior to contraction the roots swell and the cells elongate. During the contraction, phase the cells in the roots contract, pulling the plant downward. The swelling phase, which takes place during the wetter season, also displaces dirt which creates a hollow area and allows the plant to be pulled downward during the drier portion of the year when the root contracts. Contractile roots are capable of exerting a tremendous amount of pulling pressure.

The contractile root keeps the plant anchored in the soil by countering the upward growth of the stem.

Chapter 7 Haustorial Roots

A haustorium is an organ of a parasite that penetrates its host and steals water and nutrients. Haustorial roots are above ground, or aerial, roots which parasitic plants produce to penetrate the host plant's tissues. Using these invasive roots, the parasitic plant absorbs the food it needs for survival. Parasitic plants usually have their own root system. These roots form a structure called a haustorium to penetrate the host's vascular tissue. The haustorium consists of a host attachment structure, a vascular infection peg, and thin filaments that infiltrate the host vascular bundles. The filaments produced by the haustorial root may penetrate the xylem and the phloem of the host plant. It manages to do this in a way that keeps the host unaware of its existence, hence unable to fight off the parasite.

Mistletoe and dodder are two prime examples of parasitic plants with haustorial roots. The mistletoe is a form of parasitic plant called a hemi-parasite parasite, which simply means it has chlorophyll to manufacture its own food. It merely needs to steal the water and nutrients it needs from the host. The dodder is an obligate parasite, as it needs everything it needs to maintain life provided by its host. Both plants use haustorial roots to obtain these from their host plant.

Most parasitic plants walk a balance between stealing enough nutrients from their host to maintain life and killing the host, and thus themselves.

Chapter 8 Propogative Roots

Propagative roots are a type of adventitious roots that form, allowing plants to propagate themselves. Strawberries and spider plants commonly form them on the bottom tips of the stolons they send out. propagative roots form at the axils of the stem and leaf. The roots also occur on philodendron plants and many others. Many grasses also form stolons that are underground, allowing the plant to extend itself for several inches to several feet away.

Propagative roots also form when gardeners and plant propagators "root" plant cuttings. Place stem, tip or root cuttings in soil media and put the container in a humid environment. Under proper conditions many plants will form, propagative roots on the portion of the plant placed underground, forming a clone of the original plant. This process is a form of propagation called vegetative propagation and is an important process for reproducing plants.

Propagative roots also form in a process called layering in which one buries a portion of the stem of a plant, usually a tip. Propagative roots form along the buried portion of the plant, producing a new plant. This process works for many vine plants like wisteria and many shrubs. Blackberries and raspberries will form propagative roots on buried stem tips.

Chapter 9 Storage Root or Root Tuber

Many plants form tuberous roots, which serve as food depositories. The food, in the form of carbohydrates, is manufactured by the plant leaves during the summer season and stored in the large, underground organ called the storage root or root tuber. The carbohydrates thus stored allow the plant to survive during the cold months when the plant cannot manufacture any food.

The outside structure of a root tuber consists of the proximal end, which is the portion of the root closest to the plant and the distal end that is the end of the root. The rootstalk is the portion that attaches the root to the plant stem at the node. Adventitious buds form along the surface, or skin, of the root tuber.

The root tuber consists of four distinct layers. The outer layer, or skin, protects the root and has the ability to form buds. The cortex is the next layer. The cambium forms the third layer. This section of the root tuber has latex vessels that transport the food manufactured by the plant to the root, and the water and nutrients gathered by the roots to the plant leaves.

A root tuber has another function other than food storage. That function is propagation. Many root tubers also form adventitious shoots that in turn form adventitious roots, allowing the plant to spread.

Many of the plants that form root tubers have become important food sources for humans. Sweet potato, cassava and yam are the most obvious examples of these crops. Animals and insects also use storage roots as a source of food.

Other plants form a sort of combination of stem/root storage system. These do not form adventitious shoots. Examples of these types of storage roots are found in the food crops carrots, beets, parsnips, radishes, and turnips.

Many biennial flowers like hollyhocks form root tubers to store food during the first year's growth to use to get a head start during the second, flower and seed-producing season. Perennial plants like dahlias and daylilies form tuberous roots to allow them to store food manufactured by the leaves during the winter months.

Propagate plants that form tuberous, or storage, roots in the autumn. Dig the roots after top growth has slowed. Divided and replant them. The new plant, as long as a section of the top crown has been included, will grow the next season, forming a new plant.

Chapter 11 Surface Roots

When someone speaks of surface roots, they are usually referring to tree roots that have grown across the surface of the ground. Although most trees will send some large roots down deep to stabilize and anchor the tree, most tree roots appear within the first four to eight inches of soil. The reason for this is that roots need oxygen in the soil to grow and perform their duties of gathering water and nutrients. Deeper soil contains less oxygen than shallow soil. Trees that grow over ten inches in diameter will tend to grow surface roots in greater abundance than smaller trees. Hard, compacted sub soils tend to discourage deeper root growth. Water saturated subsoil will also encourage surface growth of roots. Sometimes soil erosion will erode soil away, exposing the roots and creating surface roots. Another reason for the appearance of surface roots is simply the growth pattern of the root. As the root grows what formerly was an underground root, close to the surface, becomes a surface root because of its greater girth.

Once surface roots appear in your lawn or cracking your sidewalk there are few remedies short of either tolerating the roots or removing the tree and replacing it with a species that is less prone to surface root growth. Several remedies can provide short-term relief. A root barrier of plastic or landscape fabric, then covered with mulch may provide some temporary relief. Over time, though, roots will find a way through the barrier and once again, the tree roots will spread over the surface. Covering the roots with an inch or so of soil and seeding with grass may also solve the problem for a short while. Eventually, though roots will grow up through this soil layer. To avoid harming the roots don't use more than a covering of two inches.

Another solution, not recommended, is to prune or cut the surface roots. Although cutting one or two roots will probably not harm the tree, excessive root pruning will lead to die back amongst the branches, weakening and probably eventually causing death for the tree. If possible, plant a perennial ground cover like pachysandra, ajuga or other under the tree and avoid mowing the area. Trying to mow this area is not good for either the mower or the tree.

Trees, which have a tenancy to grow surface roots, include:

Most maples (except Japanese Maple), American Beech, European Larch, Sweet Gum, Dawn Redwood, White

Mulberry, Colorado Blue Spruce, Poplars, Pin Oak, White Willow, Bald Cypress and Lindens (Basswood) and locusts.

Trees that are less likely to grow surface roots include:

Japanese Maple, Red Buckeye Juneberry, Hornbeams, Dogwoods, Hawthorns, European Beech, Sourwood, and Bur Oaks.

Note that these trees, under the right circumstances, may still produce surface roots but since most of these trees are of the smaller variety, the roots should be smaller and less troublesome if they appear.

Chapter 12 Rooting Plant Cuttings

Many plants have the ability to form adventitious roots from the stem or leaf. This ability allows gardeners and professional plant propagators to reproduce their favorite garden plants by using a process called rooting cuttings. Though procedures for each plant species may be slightly different, general conditions for producing cuttings from plants are similar.

To produce rooted cuttings from most plants you will need:

Good quality soil potting media

A pot to put the media in

Place a clear plastic sheet over the pot to admit light and increase humidity

Labels

Cutting material

The basic procedure is similar for each plant from which you wish to propagate by rooting cuttings. You choose a section of the branch, usually about two to six inches long. There should be at least two leaf joints on this section. Strip the lower leaves off the lower leaf axils. If you wish to use a rooting hormone, now is the time. Place the hormone on the lower portion of the plant cutting. Stick the cutting into the media firm the soil media around it. Label the cutting as to what it is and the date it was stuck. If you are using a large pot, you should, using bent wire or some other contrivance, suspend the plastic over the cutting and secure it around the pot with a rubber band or string so it covers the cuttings tightly without touching them.

Keep the humidity high in the rooting chamber by frequent misting and watering. Place in an area of bright light, but keep out of the direct sun. Under a tree or on the north side of a house or building is ideal. If you have a lot of cuttings to produce you may use a cold frame or hot bed. Use of a plant mister to produce a light spray of misty water will increase the number of successful cuttings and decrease the time required for rooting to occur.

The time required for rooting cuttings varies by species of plants. Some easy to root species like most annual and perennial flowers, may be rooted in two weeks. Shrubs and trees may take much longer. Once rooting is complete the new plant, called a clone, may be planted in a larger pot and grown to a larger size before setting out in the garden.

Annual flowers that are easily rooted:

Fibrous Begonia

Geranium (Pelargonium)

Coleus

Impatiens

Perennial Flowers Which May Be Rooted:

Asters

Chrysanthemums

Iberis

Vegetables From Rooting Cuttings

Tomato

Pepper

Sweet Potato

Shrubs Which May Be Rooted for Cuttings

Viburnum

Yew

Privet

Juniper

Alberta Spruce

Lilac

Euonymus

Fruits Which May be Rooted for Cuttings

Grapes

Blackberries

Raspberries

Rooting your own cuttings to produce more plants for your garden or friends is a fun way to expand your gardening skills.

Gardener's Guide To Making Compost For the Garden

Make Your Own Compost - A Quick How to Guide

Making compost is easy and this quick how to guide will help you make compost fast.

Making your own compost is not a complex operation. However, there are many different ways of making compost and the one you choose is dependent upon the type of materials you have and the time you can devote to tending the compost pile.

The first step in making your own compost is choosing the location of the compost pile. If you are using an enclosed compost bin, like a barrel or tumbler, you may want it somewhere where it is handy to get to, but out of sight. Wherever you put it, make sure you can get to it easily for loading and unloading. If using an open bin, like a wire enclosure, you may want to consider devoting a small area of the garden for the compost pile. One could move the pile each year so the nutrients that leach out of the pile will be available in the garden soil below it. If you are using an open bin compost pile, put a layer of shredded leaves or straw on the soil to provide some drainage.

Making your own compost using the so-called "hot" method is the most labor-intensive method of making compost. It will give you good quality compost quickly. For a hot compost pile, you will need to assemble all the materials before building the pile. You will want to use about one third "green" materials like grass clipping and fresh kitchen scraps. For best results, you will need at least a cubic yard of material for the pile. Use a shredder to chop up large materials. You will want about two-thirds "brown" materials like shredded leaves or straw. You may also mix in organic materials like wood ashes, cottonseed meal, seaweed extract, and blood meal. Layer the materials, green, brown, green brown. Put a small amount of garden soil between the layers, if you want. A compost thermometer will help you monitor the temperature. This type of compost pile will need turning weekly. Use a compost turner, pitchfork, or garden fork. When it is finished, the compost pile needs to cure a bit before using. The total time to make this type of compost is about eight weeks.

If you want to make your own compost, but don't want to go to all that trouble, you can use the "cold" compost method. In this method, you may use the compost materials as they become available to you. Locate the compost pile, and then put a layer of dry material in the bottom, like shredded leaves or straw. Then just add kitchen scraps and garden refuse as they become available. Add the new material to the center of the pile. Occasionally you will want to rake the material in the center to the edges, creating a slight depression in the center to which you continue to add material. A small amount of garden soil added occasionally helps keep things composting. You really don't need to turn this type of pile, and it probably will not heat up. It will take longer to make compost using this method.

You can also use earthworms to make compost. Using special bins that stack one on top of another, worms digest between five and eight pounds of kitchen scraps each week and will produce a bin of finished compost a month. The worms will naturally migrate from one bin to another as they consume the food into a fresh bin placed above them. Some composting tips:

Use only vegetable matter in making your compost pile. Bones and meat waste will stink and attract pests.

If the compost pile does develop a foul odor, it needs air. Aerating the pile should eliminate the odor. Adding lime or covering the pile with soil should stop the odor too.

Use a compost keeper in the kitchen to collect the compost. Empty it periodically into the compost pile. This will minimize the trips to the compost pile in bad weather or at night.

Use a compost sifter to screen finished compost to screen out large pieces that did not compost. The gardener may add this material to another compost pile for further breakdown.

Compost Activator - Jump Starter for Your Compost Pile

A compost activator will trigger a compost pile to start breaking down quicker and forming a rich soil additive for your soil faster. These activators will all contain a different mix of ingredients. These ingredients will run the gamut from soil fungus and bacteria additives, which are natural organisms, found in all healthy soils. These microscopic organisms will help activate the compost pile and start it rotting away.

Other ingredients possibly included in a compost activator will be nitrogen rich ingredients like blood meal, cottonseed meal, alfalfa meal and soybean meal. Seaweed meals of different types may also be included in these starter blends. If you decide to use a compost activator in your compost pile, be sure to read the instructions thoroughly. These mixes are not cheap and you don't want to waste your money by misusing the product.

Normal garden soil contains all the ingredients you need to get a compost pile started, so if you can incorporate a little bit of soil in the compost heap, you will be adding the microorganisms you need to act as an activator for your compost pile. You can add the nitrogen needed by these microorganisms by adding green material, such as grass clippings, to the pile.

A compost activator may not be necessary to get your compost pile started. However, if you want compost quicker, it may be best to add one. These products do contain all the ingredients to help your compost pile going faster and will digest the compost pile ingredients more efficiently. Keep in mind the fact that if your compost pile contains the large amount of nitrogen rich (green) materials, you will need to add less of the activator.

Compost Bins, Barrels and Pails

You will find a wide assortment of different kinds of compost bins, barrels and pails to suit just about any need. Most of these are suitable for either hot or cold compost.

Use compost pails for short term compost storage. Normal use is in the kitchen or other storage area in the home. Throw kitchen scraps in them on a daily basis. When full add the contents to the compost pile. This helps avoid daily trips to the compost pile when you do not have time, or when the weather is bad.

Compost bins can be as simple as the knock down wire compost bins. These are great for temporary compost bins. Use them to store leaves over the winter for use in the spring as mulch. They may also find use to compost garden materials. Typically, these have steel pins that insert in the corners. The pins extend down into the ground, anchoring them in place.

Compost barrels are enclosed containers that have screened holes to admit air, but not rodents. They are usually dark colored to absorb more solar energy to help heat up the compost, causing it to break down faster.

Compost Sifter

Use a compost sifter, or sieve, to screen the large, un-composted bits of material from your compost pile.

Sometimes not all the material you put in the compost bin digests by the time you want to use the compost. This can include sticks, large plant stems, and other large debris left behind. This material can be screened out by using a compost sifter, or sieve. Add the resulting fine compost material to a seedbed or garden. Add the material that did not compost to another pile.

A compost sieve will usually have a one-quarter inch screen that serves as the sifter, fastened to a box that will then fit over a bucket or wheelbarrow. Shovel the compost into the sifter. Shake the sifter, and the fine material will fall through. Add the larger left over material to another compost pile for further composting.

Compost Thermometer

Maintaining the correct temperature in a compost pile is important, and a compost thermometer will help you determine that.

A compost thermometer is used to check the temperature of a compost pile to make sure it is at the correct level of between ninety and one hundred forty degrees Fahrenheit. If the temperature is lower than that, proper digestion of the materials may not take place. Hotter than that and there is the possibility that the beneficial microorganisms within it will be killed. A too hot pile also runs the danger of spontaneous combustion, as sometimes happens to farmers who bale hay that is too green.

Compost Tumbler

Speed up the composting process with a compost tumbler.

A compost tumbler makes good compost fast. You will find four types of compost tumbler, each with its own advantages and disadvantages.

A sphere tumbler is a big hollow ball that you fill with the compost material and roll around in your yard mixing the ingredients. Some of these models have bases to sit on, allowing the sphere to stay in one place while you roll it. These types may be hard to unload once the compost is finished.

The center axle mounted compost tumbler is the most common type found in the home garden. These tumblers usually have two doors, which makes loading and unloading easier. In many cases, a wheelbarrow fits directly under one of the doors and the compost emptied directly into the wheelbarrow for spreading. The center axle usually has some type of aerators on it, which help mix air into the compost, allowing it to digest properly.

A rolling drums compost tumbler sits horizontally on a base that is equipped with rollers or bearings for the drum to rotate. These can be harder than other types to load and unload. The gardener may remove some of these from the base to load them. Sometimes the gardener can move the tumbler to the garden and dump the compost right in the spot that that requires the compost. However, keep in mind that a compost tumbler loaded with compost will be heavy, and difficult to roll.

Most gardeners consider the hand crank tumbler top of the line tumbler, as they are quite pricy. A crank controls the rolling action. The drum mounts on a frame. Turning these units is usually very easy. The compost mixes using internal baffles that mix and aerate the compost materials. These are a bit harder to load, but may be unloaded in a fashion similar to the center axle type. One model, the Mantiss 4000 twin, has two chambers. You fill one chamber while the one is composting. When one side is finished, you empty it and fill it, while the other is working.

The operation of tumbler compost makers is the same, though there will be differences between the models and manufacturers. Be sure to read the instructions fully. Add the ingredients to the tumbler and turn it daily to mix them to produce uniform compost. They are rodent proof as they are fully enclosed. It is also difficult for small children to get into them, as well as pets. They are usually attractive, and do not look objectionable on or near a patio. Since they are enclosed, composting odors are not free to stink up the yard.

Compost Turner

In order to be broken down completely, compost needs combine thoroughly with air to allow the microbes to breath. The use of a compost turners, or aerators, will accomplish this task. There are two basic types of these garden tools.

The T-handle compost turner is usually around thirty-six inches long. The handles are on the top, forming a t shape. An augur type blade on the bottom bores into the mix using a twisting motion. When the blade has penetrated to the bottom of the mix, you pull upward. This action mixes the compost, performing an aerator function by mixing in air.

The adjustable handle compost turner has two handles, one on the top, the other about six inches from the end of the tool. The handles on this aerator tool are adjustable for either right or left-handed operation. These types work a bit different from the t handle. There are folding wings located at the bottom of the tool that folds up tight to the body when they are plunged into the compost. When you pull up, the wings flip out, mixing and aerating the compost.

Kitchen Compost Keeper Pail

A compost keeper is a pail designed to minimize those trips to the compost pile. These pails are small, usually only designed to hold about one gallon or so of refuse.

The compost keeper works great to put coffee grounds, eggshells, vegetable parings and other kitchen scraps in to save trips out to the compost pile. When the pail is full, you can make just one trip to the compost pile instead of several.

Some compost keepers are equipped with charcoal filters to eliminate the odors of the kitchen scraps held inside them. These last around six months and replacement filters should be available to replace them.

Use the compost keeper only to store scraps in temporarily, not to make the compost.

Trench Composting

Trench composting is the simplest system of composting the gardener can choose. The basics of trench composting are simple; you dig a trench or hole, toss in kitchen scraps, weeds and crop residue, then cover it with soil and dig another trench.

The trench can be any size; the only suggestion is that it be about twelve inches deep. Save the dirt in buckets or other receptacle for covering the last trench if there are to be a number of trenches. After digging the trench, which can be any width, many gardeners only excavate an area the width of the shovel, use the shovel to break up the soil at the bottom of the trench. At this point a the gardener may add a mineral soil supplement such as greensand, phosphate rock, wood ash or other long term soil supplement into this layer.

Add vegetative matter to the trench. This can be kitchen scraps, coffee grounds, non-woody plant trimmings, crop residue and weeds. When about a six to eight inch layer of organic material has accumulated use the shovel to chop it up. This step is not necessary, but it will help the vegetative material break down faster.

Cover the vegetative matter with a layer of soil that can be from an adjacent area of the garden or the soil taken out earlier. The trench will now be a mound that will settle at a somewhat higher level than it was after the vegetative matter has decomposed.

Trench composting works well with any type of gardening but works especially well with raised bed gardening. Using this system for raised beds does not require taking an area out of production. Simply dig short trenches in harvested areas and fill with garden waste during the week. Once a week add kitchen scraps, which have accumulated in the kitchen in a compost pail, then, cover the trench and dig a new one. The gardener may plant the area above the trench about two weeks after covering.

Dig trenches between the rows in a row garden while the garden is in production, or the gardener may take an area out of production for a year.

A standard English system is to use a three years system that divides the garden into three-foot wide beds. In Year One, the gardener digs a one-foot wide trench to use to discard garden waste. A ribbon of soil next to the trench becomes the planting bed and another ribbon of soil between the two becomes a walking path. In Year Two dig the soil from the walking path onto the previous year's trench and use it for the walkway. The excavated pathway becomes the new trench with the planting bed in the area that was the walkway the previous year. In year three the walkway from Year Two becomes the planting bed and the gardener excavates Year Two's planting bed becomes the new trench.

Gardeners in housing developments that have rules against composting can usually trench compost if they fill the trench in on a weekly basis and it does not become an eyesore or a magnet for critters. Dig a trench in harvested areas in raised beds and fill with crop residue and kitchen waste. Planting can follow within two to three weeks after the compost have been covered.

Trench composting has several advantages. The decomposing compost lies at the very place that the plants need it, right under their roots. There should be little or no odor, especially with smaller beds that the gardener digs and covers frequently. The enterprising gardener can even enlist a posthole digger to excavate small holes in the actively growing garden, between perennials and shrubs in an ornamental planting or near trees. Take care around trees and shrubs. The holes or trenches should be just outside the drip line to avoid damaging roots.

Any type of vegetative matter can serve as fodder for trench composting. It is a great way to dispose of autumn leaves or grass clippings. Add the entire crop residue from the garden to the trench as well as non-woody shrub and tree trimmings. The gardener may add woody material if it is first run through a chipper/shredder to break it down.

Use Worms to Make Your Compost

Worms can break down vegetable matter fast into a high quality compost mix.

Using worms to create compost for your garden is a great idea. Worms can digest just about any vegetable waste from your kitchen and create high quality compost that has a lot of nutrients.

Composting with worms using a specially made worm compost bin is a straightforward project. The worm compost bins are stacked, one on top of another. When one bin is full of refuse, place another one on top of it. Introduce worms to the bottom bin, which consume the vegetable matter in it. They will then migrate up to the next bin on their own. You can then use the compost in the bin they have vacated. Refill the emptied bin with refuse and place it on top of the other one to repeat the cycle.

Some worm compost bins have another feature that allows you to use the liquid waste produced by the worms. Called worm tea, this liquid is great to water plants with after drawing it off. A worm composting operation can consume five to eight pounds of food a week and produce one bin a month of compost.

What is Worm Composting?

Worm composting, or vermiculture, involves feeding kitchen and garden wastes to red worms. The wrigglers consume it and produce a brown, peat-like material called castings. These castings are a nutrient rich soil additive for the vegetable or flower garden.

Benefits of Vermiculture

Worm composting provides gardeners with several benefits, which include:

Properly done, worm bins are odorless

A worm farm takes little space

Organic worm castings can reduce chemical fertilizer use in the garden.

The castings are suitable for adding to lawns, flower gardens and potted plant containers.

The Life of a Worm

Those little round wrigglers have an interesting sex life. Worms are hermaphrodites, which is a fancy way of saying that each worm has both male and female sex organs. Near the head of the worm is a white band called a clitellum that contains the worm's sex organs. Worms still must find another worm to reproduce. Two mating worms join with their heads facing opposite directions. Sperm pass between them, fertilizing each other's eggs.

Cocoons, each holding up to five eggs, form on the clitellum. The cocoons detach and hatch when soil conditions are suitable. The eggs can survive for years.

When they eggs hatch, the tiny white worms begin to feed immediately. Worms mature in about four to six weeks. Worms can live for many years under the right conditions. Earthworm bodies comprise about ninety percent water. When they do die, they decay quickly, becoming part of the soil that sustained them.

What to Feed the Worms

Red worms can eat just about any kind of vegetable matter, including:

Fruit and potato peels

Spoiled lettuce scraps

Napkins, paper towels

Corrugated cardboard (shredded)

They don't want any meat, bone, gristle, or dairy products. Strong waste like onion or garlic skins doesn't work out well for them either. Layer in some garden soil to give the worms some grit to aid digestion.

How Many Worms Do You Need?

If you want the worms to compost all the output from your kitchen, save the waste for a week and weigh it. A worm will consume about one-half its body weight a day. A pound of worms contains about 500 wrigglers. That many worms could consume about three and a half pounds of waste a week. If you produce four pounds of scraps a week, you will need about 500 worms.

What Kind of Worms Should You Use?

For best results use commercial red worms. Don't use night crawlers, as they need to burrow deep in the soil, so they won't usually survive in a worm bin. Garden red worms are not adapted to life in a worm bin. Get the worms by ordering online, or buy some from a bait shop.

The Worm Castings

Worm castings, or Vermicompost, are an excellent fertilizer. Vermicompost contains:

Beneficial soil microbes

A High Concentration of plant nutrients

Organic matter

Growth regulators that enhance plant growth

University studies show that using worm castings may increase yields of many vegetable crops. Worm castings contain from five to eleven times the concentrations of phosphorus, nitrogen and potassium than the soil they ingest.

Types of Worm Compost Bins

There are several types of worm compost systems, the most common being the standard worm bin which is the simplest to build. The worms will last for months in a good size bin before the castings need harvesting. A continuous flow worm farm is another popular option. In this system, you add vegetable matter at the top. The worms feed on the decaying vegetable matter, breaking it down. The castings drop out of a slatted bottom into a collection bin for harvest.

For gardeners composting with red worms can solve several problems. The worms provide a convenient way dispose of kitchen waste and produce a nutrient rich fertilizer for the garden in the process. Bring on the worms.

About the Author

Gardening, history and travel seem an odd soup in which to stew one's life, but Paul has done just that. A gardener since 1975, he has spent his spare time reading history and traveling with his wife. He gardens, plans his travels and writes his books out in the sticks near a small town in southeast Indiana. He enjoys sharing the things he has learned about gardening, history and travel with his readers. The many books Paul has written reflect that joy of sharing. He also writes fiction in his spare time. Read and enjoy his books, if you will. Or dare.

Now, back to writing, if he can get the cat off the keyboard.

Join Paul on Facebook

Twitter

paulwonning@gmail.com

Mossy Feet Books Catalog

To Get Your Free Copy of the Mossy Feet Books Catalogue, Click This <u>Link</u>**.**

Gardening Books

Fantasy Books

Humor

Science Fiction

Semi – Autobiographical Books

Travel Books

The Hawaiian Chronicles – Our Hawaiian Adventures

Episode I - The Journey Begins

Paul R. Wonning

To celebrate our 25th wedding anniversary the wife and I ventured to our 50th state. Many hours of planning and deliberation went into this journey. Our first debates centered on the method of transportation. I wanted to drive while the wife felt an airplane might be better. Much discussion centered on this controversy, and I am chagrined to admit I finally had to relent. Hours of research led me to believe that there is no highway to Hawaii, a serious omission on the part of our road builders. No road, no car! The wife was right, we had to fly.

So now that we had determined our mode of travel, what to do upon arrival? The wife wanted to sightsee! You know, actually drive around and look at things! Just like a couple of tourists. My idea was to hang out at the beach and look cool, just like they do on Baywatch. The wife made some snide remarks about my unique physique. The remarks intimated that it was not conducive to looking cool on the beach, which led to more discussions. Our negotiations soon centered on a cruise or a dogsled tour. The wife seemed to think that there weren't any dogsleds on Hawaii, so the Hawaiian Cruise won out.

We would tour the Hawaiian Islands aboard the ship SS Independence of the American Cruise Lines. The tour would include four islands and five ports in seven days. Beginning on Maui in the port of Kahalui on Sunday the ship would proceed to the port of Hilo on the island of Hawaii, the Big Island. We would spend Monday in Hilo. It would then proceed to the Kona Coast port of Kailua on Tuesday. Wednesday and Thursday, we would spend on the island of Oahu in the port of Honolulu. Friday's destination would be Nawilili on the island of Kauai. Saturday we would return to Maui

for the flight home.

The AAA travel agency in Columbus, Indiana handled our travel arrangements. Our itinerary included:

Cincinnati

Ohio

Dallas

Texas

Los Angeles

California

Honolulu

Hawaii

Kahalui

Packing and other preparatory arrangements were a nightmare. The wife wanted to pack scads of clothing. I said, hell, everyone in Hawaii walks around in swimming trunks and flip-flops, we don't need any clothes. She said I been to too many Jimmy Buffet concerts, which led to more discussions. Which I lost. Again. In the weeks before departure, the wife was in a frenzy of activity - shopping and picking out clothes to take. There were clothes hanging all over the house. They hung on doors, chairs, and chandeliers. Shoot, I went to sleep watching a basketball game and awoke to find six pairs of pants and some shirts hanging from my big toe. On the day of departure, we had twenty-five suitcases, six duffels, three backpacks, her purse and my wallet. I said this seemed a little extreme as we only had two backs, how could we use three backpacks. I actually won this point! EEEhah!

The day of our departure finally arrived on February 17, 2001. Our initial flight was out of Cincinnati, Ohio on Comair Flight 6009 to Dallas, Texas at 7:00 AM. Anyone that flies a lot probably hates it. However, this was only my second flight by commercial airline and I thoroughly enjoyed the experience. We have done a fair amount of traveling, but always by car. The take off was smooth, the sunrise above the clouds just spectacular. I am amazed at how hard the flight attendants work rolling the cart up and down the aisle - always with a smile. We arrived above Dallas about 9:30, landing at 9:45. This is, as all times will be for the flight out, Indiana Time. Dallas looks nice from the air. There must have been heavy rains as the rivers and streams looked flooded. We breakfasted at the airport, and then departed Dallas at 11:25 AM for Los Angeles on Delta Flight 2119. I had a window seat so I had a good view of the landscape underneath until we got to the Rockies. Since clouds now obscured the view, we passed the time reading.

Arrival in LA was around 2:30 PM. Here we had a rather lengthy layover so we ate, read, and slept. We finally boarded the plane for Hawaii at 5:45 PM. Delta Flight 1579 left LA at 6:15 PM for Honolulu, Hawaii. The view of the receding California coast was the last thing we would see for a while, as the sky over the Pacific was mostly cloudy. Seeing the mainland slip away was both exciting and scary.

When the plane began its descent to the islands, it was about 11:30 PM Indiana time. This is about 6:30 PM Hawaii time, so it was still daylight. We passed over the island of Oahu and started our approach to Honolulu International Airport. Honolulu is impressive from the air at night. The city is lit up above the sparkling Pacific waters. The volcanic mountains constitute a striking backdrop. It is a beautiful sight.

Although we were flying on the same plane from Honolulu to Kahului, we had to leave the plane so they could clean it. I told the flight attendants that the wife enjoyed cleaning. Would the consider a discount on the far if she vacuumed while I finished my nap? While the attendant considered this request, my shin developed a rather sharp pain. Needles to say, we left the plane. The flight crew noticed my limp.

We departed Honolulu for Kahului at about 1:00 AM. It was completely dark now, so we could see nothing of the island below us except lights. All our flights that day had been smooth, so the flight from Honolulu to Kahluiu was memorable for its uniqueness. The plane passed over two mountain ranges, and I swear the plane hit every mountain in them both. Moreover, they didn't fully pressurize the plane's cabin. My head felt like an over inflated basketball on the way up, and like the inside of a flushed toilet on the way down.

We landed at Kahului at 1:30 AM (Indiana Time) - 8:30 PM Hawaii time. Representatives of the American Hawaiian

Cruise line met us at the airport. They collected our luggage, which by this time was in much better shape than we were. They herded us on a bus and took us to the port for check-in. Here another representative of the Line greeted us. By this time, my head felt like someone had stuck it in a jug, sucked out all the air, and then smashed the jug with a hammer. OOOh the joys of air travel. By 2:00 AM, nineteen hours after leaving winter in Indiana, we were in the tropics! The Cruise Line had a special lunch prepared for arrivals. We ate, found our way back to our stateroom somehow, and immediately fell asleep. Welcome to Hawaii!

NOTE: *This trip occurred in 2001. Sadly, the American Cruise Lines has gone out of business and the SS Independence to the scrap heap.*

Mossy Feet Books

Printed in Great Britain
by Amazon